HAMLYN · COLOURFAX · SERIES

fun with

SCIENCE

ROBIN KERROD

CONTENTS

Introduction	2
A kaleidoscope of colour	3
Heave two	6
Fizz and snuffle	7
Test your senses	8
Scaling the Moon and the Sun	10
Sounds better	11
Invisible influence	12
Magic boats	14
Deep breaths	16
Hear your heart	17
Air pressure tricks	18
It's easy to see	19
Ring tin-tin	20
Water spinner	21
Keeping a weather eye	22
Getting the wind up	24
Plop and glow	26
Compass needles	27
Magnet magic	28
Di, di, dit, dah, dah, dah, di, di dit	30
Index	32

HAMLYN

INTRODUCTION

Welcome fellow scientists! Here is a book full of experiments, activities – and a few tricks – to introduce you to the exciting world of science. By working through the experiments, you will learn about science in the best possible way – by doing things yourself. The text explains how to set up the experiments, and tells you what should happen and why. How? what? and why? are questions scientists ask and have to answer all the time.

Most of the things you need for the experiments, such as tins, jars, paper, candles and sticky tape, you can find around the home. Others, such as magnets and lenses, you will be able to buy quite cheaply at a hobby shop or hardware store. It's a good idea to keep all your experimental equipment together in a box or cupboard. Then you won't have to chase around looking for it every time you want to do an experiment. And it won't get in other people's way!

When you carry out experiments, always keep notes about the things you use (apparatus), what you do (method), and what happens (observations and results). All scientists do this. If an experiment doesn't work first time, don't be discouraged. Try again. You may find there is something simple you haven't done. By doing things wrong, you sometimes learn more than when you do things right! Good experimenting!

SAFETY FIRST

The experiments in this book should be great fun. And you will always learn a lot about the science too. But before you start, remember a few "dos" and "don'ts".

Always ask permission from your parents or another adult before trying any of the experiments. Ask their advice if you do not understand what to do. Make sure you have all the equipment you need before you start. Be particularly careful in experiments with lighted candles. In these experiments always make sure a parent or another adult is nearby in case of accidents. In some experiments you will need to use a hammer and nails and occasionally a drill. Again, ask your parents if you can use them first, and watch your fingers!

Other safety dos and don'ts:
- DO wear an apron to protect your clothes.
- DON'T touch anything hot with your bare hands.
- DON'T use tins with jagged edges.
- DO carry out experiments with water over a sink or outside.
- DO wash your hands after every experiment.
- DON'T leave everything in a mess when you have finished!

DANGER SYMBOL

Look for this warning symbol. In experiments marked with this symbol, you will need to ask an adult to help you and stay with you throughout the experiment.

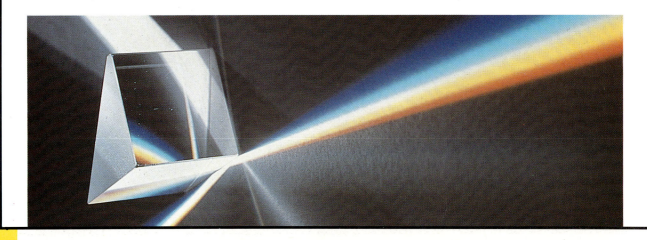

A KALEIDOSCOPE OF COLOUR

You will need: 2 mirrors ● card ● sticky tape ● greaseproof paper ● sugar crystals ● torch

The kaleidoscope has been a favourite toy for over 170 years. Kaleidoscope means "seeing beautiful shapes", and the name tells you what it does. When you look through it, you see colourful patterns that are symmetrical, or look the same from any direction. They are pictures produced by mirrors.

You can make a simple kaleidoscope quite easily. You need two mirrors of the same size, long and narrow ones if possible. Tape them together along one long side, both facing in the same direction. Now tape between them a piece of card the same size as one of the mirrors, so you get a triangular shape.

Tape a piece of greaseproof paper over one end, then turn it the other way up. Drop in the middle of the triangle some coloured sugar crystals or a few bits of coloured paper. Cover up the open end with paper, and cut a small hole in the middle for viewing. The kaleidoscope is now ready. Shine a torch up through the greaseproof-paper end, and look through the viewing hole. You'll see beautiful colour patterns. Shake the kaleidoscope and the patterns will change.

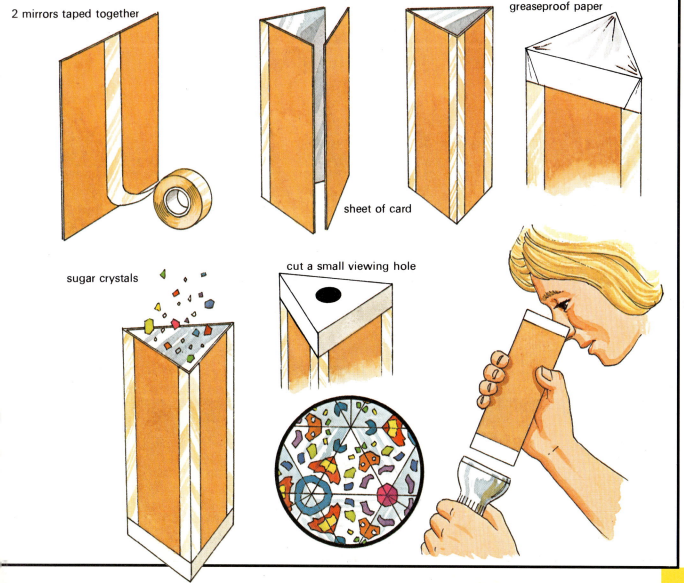

2 mirrors taped together

sheet of card

greaseproof paper

sugar crystals

cut a small viewing hole

SPREADING COLOURS

You will need: blotting paper • coloured ink • 2 glass jars • card

If you enjoy painting, you will know that you can make new colours by mixing together different coloured paints. For example, you can make green by mixing together yellow and blue. In the same way you can make new colours by mixing together different coloured inks. In fact most of the inks in bottles and in felt-tip pens are mixtures of different coloured dyes. You can find out which in this experiment.

Take a strip of blotting paper, and drip a few drops of, for example, black ink near one end. Suspend the paper from a pencil so that this end dips into water in the bottom of a jar. Make sure the ink spot is above the water level.

The water will slowly rise through the blotting paper and through the ink spot.

cold water

Gradually, different colours start appearing above the spot. These are the different coloured dyes that were mixed together to make the black ink.

COLOUR SEPARATING

This method of separating colours is known as chromatography, which means "colour drawing". Chemists often use it in chemical analysis, to find what substances are present in a sample of something. They may use paper chromatography, like you do, or perform the experiment in a tube packed with suitable material. They may then pass special liquids or gases through the tube. Gas chromatography can detect the very tiniest traces of substances imaginable.

A COLOUR FOUNTAIN

You will need: jar of hot water • jar of cold water • coloured ink • card

This is a dramatic way to see colours spreading.

Fill a glass jar with hot water and add a few drops of coloured ink. Fill a second jar with cold water and, holding a piece of card over the top, carefully turn the jar upside down and place it on top of the first one. Remove the card. You will see a spectacular fountain of colour as the hot water rises into the top jar.

THE SPECTRUM

The band of colours in a rainbow is called a spectrum. You can produce a spectrum in other ways. A good way is to pass sunlight through a wedge-shaped piece of glass, known as a prism. The colours spread out as they enter and leave the faces of the glass. They do this because different colours bend by different amounts when they pass through a surface. Violet light is bent the most, red light the least.

hot coloured water

VANISHING COLOURS

You will need: card ● protractor ● crayons ● nail ● glue

You have seen how you can split up white light into a rainbow of colours. You can also do the reverse – turn the colours of the rainbow back into white light.

Cut out a disc from a piece of card and divide it up into six equal parts. Use a protractor to do this, measuring an angle of 60 degrees for each segment. Colour the segments in the order in which they appear in the rainbow – red, orange, yellow, green, blue and violet.

Push a flat-headed nail (such as a plasterboard nail) through the middle of the disc and glue it in place. When the glue has set, fix the nail in the head of a hand drill and turn the handle. As the disc spins faster and faster, the colours blend together to make white.

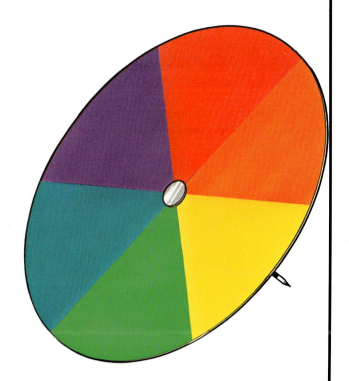

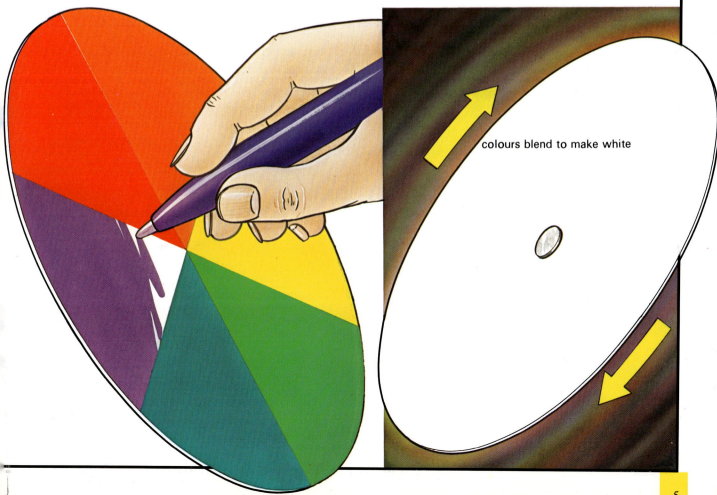

colours blend to make white

You will need: clothes line • 2 broom handles • 2 friends

How strong are you? Maybe stronger than you think. With a little help from science, you can show you are stronger than any two of your friends put together!

Give each of your friends a broom handle to hold. Tie a piece of rope (or a clothes line) to one of the handles, and wrap the rope around both the handles several times, as shown. Ask your friends to pull on the handles, while you pull on the end of the rope. Amazingly your friends will not be able to pull the handles apart. Indeed, you will be able to pull them together, no matter how hard your friends try to stop you.

This trick does not work because of your strength. It works because you have made the broom handles and rope into a pulley system – a simple device that magnifies effort, or pull. A pulley will help you to lift a heavy load with a little effort. In this case, you overcome the big pull of your two friends (the heavy load) with a little pull (the effort).

In the construction industry people use a similar kind of pulley system to lift enormous objects quite effortlessly. This system is called a block and tackle and forms the major part of a crane.

FIZZ AND SNUFFLE (X)

You will need: candle • tin • vinegar • baking soda • paper

When you want to put out a very small fire, you can pour water on it or smother it with a wet cloth. But you can also do it invisibly, using the gas that puts the fizz in fizzy drinks – carbon dioxide.

Carbon dioxide is widely used in home fire extinguishers. It can put out fires because it is heavier than air. The heavy gas pushes the air away from what is burning. But nothing can burn without the oxygen in air, so the fire is put out.

You can prove this for yourself. To represent a small fire, use a candle in a tin. Make some carbon dioxide in a large bottle by adding vinegar to one or two tablespoons of baking soda. The vinegar makes the soda fizz and give off carbon dioxide. Carefully "pour" the carbon dioxide gas from the bottle, through a rolled-up paper tube, into the tin.

You will soon find that the candle goes out. The heavy carbon dioxide gas pushes the air out of the tin and snuffs out the flame.

vinegar

baking soda

fire extinguisher

candle "snuffed" out

TEST YOUR SENSES

We have five senses in all. They include touch, sight, smell, taste and hearing. Below are some experiments to demonstrate just a few of these.

TAKING FINGERPRINTS

You will need: pencil ● paper ● sticky tape

Scribble heavily on some paper with a pencil to make a black mark. Rub your finger on it until it is quite black and then press it on to a piece of transparent sticky tape. The ridges that are on the outer layer of skin on your fingers will show up as a fingerprint. Turn the tape over and stick it to a piece of white paper to protect the print.

MAP YOUR TONGUE

You will need: salt ● sugar ● lemon juice ● coffee ● mirror ● paper ● pencil

Small organs, called taste buds, are located just below the surface of the tongue and at three places in the throat. Taste sensations can be divided into sweet, salty, sour and bitter.

Place a small amount of salt (salty taste), sugar (sweet), lemon juice (sour) and coffee (bitter) into separate saucers. Add a small amount of water to each. Now draw an outline like the one below to represent your tongue.

Look in the mirror. Dip a teaspoon in the first solution and place it on any part of your tongue. Mark on the drawing SA to show where you can taste salty. Do it again on another part of your tongue. Do the same thing for the remaining solutions. Use the letters SW for sweet, SO for sour, and BI for bitter. Don't forget to rinse your mouth out between each taste.

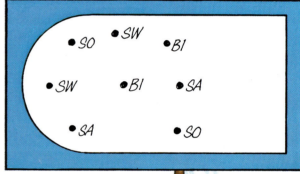

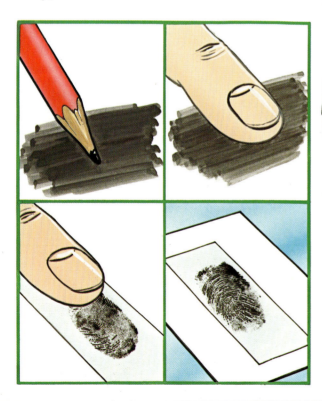

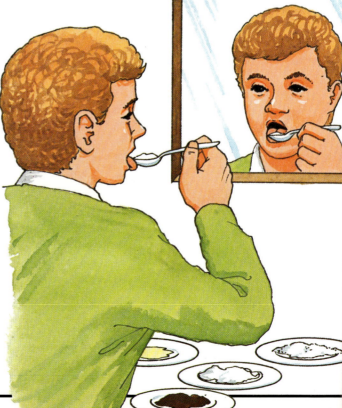

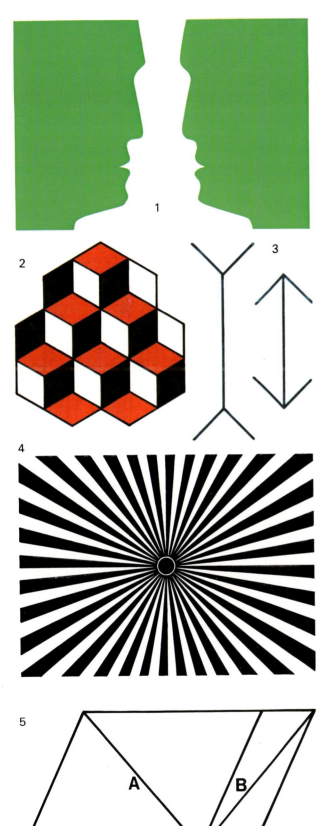

OPTICAL ILLUSIONS

Sometimes our eyes deceive us and things are not what they appear to be. Optical illusions are caused by several things. Sometimes our eyes do not look at an object properly and our brain receives misleading information. Sometimes the brain receives new information and does not know how to interpret it.

For example, can you see two heads or a candlestick in this picture (**1**)? Are the blue surfaces the bottom or the top of the cubes (**2**)? Which line is the longer (**3**) and is the pattern moving in **4**? Finally, is A longer than B (**5**)? Try some of these out on your friends.

GETTING ON YOUR NERVES

Ask someone to blindfold you and then press the point of one, two and three pencils in turn, first on your hand and then on the back of your neck. How many pencils can you feel? What do you feel if someone touches the back of your neck with a feather?

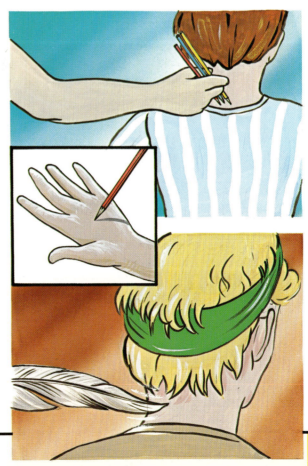

SCALING THE MOON AND THE SUN

You will need: card ● pair of compasses ● a friend

Astronomers, the scientists that study the heavens, can tell us a lot about the heavenly bodies. They tell us that the Moon is about a quarter the size of the Earth in diameter, but that the Sun is over a hundred times bigger across than the Earth. The Moon is some 385,000 km (240,000 miles) away, while the Sun is nearly 1,500,000,000 km (93,000,000 miles) away.

It is very difficult to imagine what these sizes and distances mean. There is a good way of understanding them a little better. On a piece of card use a pair of compasses to draw a circle 4 mm (0.15 in) in diameter. This represents the Earth. About 12 cm (4.5 in) away from the Earth make a dot about 1 mm (0.3 in) across. This represents the Moon the right size and distance away.

Next, draw on a big sheet of card a circle 44 cm (9 in) across. This is the Sun on the same scale as the Earth and Moon. Ask a friend to walk 48 m (156 ft) away from you and hold up the Sun disc. The Earth, Moon and Sun are now in scale in both size and distance. Notice how far away the Sun is.

OFF TO THE STARS

The Sun seems a long way from the Earth, but this is but a small step in space. The stars are much, much farther away. Even the closest (Proxima Centauri) lies over 40 million million km (25 million million miles) away. Even on the scale you have just used to show the distance to the Sun, Proxima Centauri would be 13,000 km (8,000 miles) away – almost the distance between England and Australia!

"Sun"

"Moon"

"Earth"

SOUNDS BETTER

You will need: a watch • a wooden table
How good is your hearing? Can you hear a watch ticking when it's a metre or more away? Almost certainly you can't if you listen in the ordinary way, with your ears separated from the watch by air. Air doesn't conduct (pass on) sound waves very well.

Now, place the watch on one end of a table, and hold your ear to the other end. You will then be able to hear the watch ticking very clearly. This shows that wood is a very much better conductor of sound than air.

Metals are better still. If you want to send messages around the house, you can do so by tapping on the water pipes.

SPEEDY WAVES

Sound waves travel quite slowly in air – at a speed of about 1,200 kph (760 mph). In a metal such as steel they travel at an astonishing 24,000 kph (15,000 mph)! Water is also a good sound conductor. That is why ships and submarines use soundwaves to communicate underwater. This method of communication is called sonar.

MAKE A GUITAR

You will need: shoebox • elastic bands • tacks • wood

An old cardboard shoebox and a few elastic bands are all you need to make a working guitar! Cut a hole in the lid of the box. Choose some bands of different thicknesses and tack them to the box as shown. Slot a wedge of wood in under the bands. Now play away!

INVISIBLE INFLUENCE

You will need: comb ● bits of paper ● balloons

Can you bend water? It might sound impossible, but it isn't. You can do it by using, of all things, your hair.

Comb your hair vigorously for a few seconds and move the comb near to a thin stream of water running from a tap. You will see the water bend because it is attracted by the comb. The comb can also be made to attract other things. Tiny pieces of paper, for example, can be made to jump up to it.

The comb attracts the water and paper because rubbing against your hair has made it electric. We say that it has been given an electric charge. This charge (negative) sets up an opposite electric charge (positive) in the water and paper.

The charges attract one another, so that the water bends and the bits of paper jump.

The kind of electricity produced by the comb is called static electricity. It doesn't flow through wires like ordinary electricity. You can give other materials a static electrical charge by rubbing them against wool or fur. Balloons are charged when they are rubbed against your sweater. In this state they can stick to the walls or ceiling.

Charged balloons do not always attract. Tie some string to two balloons. Rub them both against your sweater, and then hold them up by the strings. You will see the balloons push apart, or repel one another. This is because they both have the same electric charge.

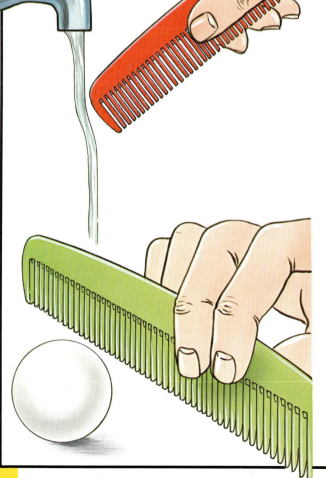

JUST FOR THE RECORD

You will need: old LP • glass • cloth • silver foil

A long-playing disc (LP) can be charged with static electricity by rubbing it vigorously with a woollen cloth. Place it on a glass. The glass will act as an insulator and stop the static electricity on the disc leaking away. Throw a few crumpled pieces of silver foil on to the disc (the little silver balls used to decorate cakes will work just as well).

The balls will start dancing about all over the disc. This happens because they become electrically charged themselves as they touch the disc. And because they have the same electric charge, they repel one another. That is what sets them moving.

OVERCHARGED

The violent movements of the air, water drops and ice particles in thunderclouds sets up static electricity. This can build up to a very high voltage (pressure), often millions of volts. When this happens, the clouds are no longer able to hold the electricity. It escapes and zig-zags down to the ground in a white-hot flash. This is lightning. The air along the flash expands suddenly with a bang as it is heated. This is the noise we hear as thunder.

You can control the balls leaping about. Try holding a plastic pen and a comb near the balls. What happens? Charge up the pen and comb by rubbing them on your hair or sweater. How do the balls react now?

Your pet cat (if you have one) can also be charged with static electricity. In a cool, dark room gently rub its fur for several minutes, always in the same direction. You will see sparks of electricity jump from the coat and you may hear the fur crackle, too. But your cat will feel nothing.

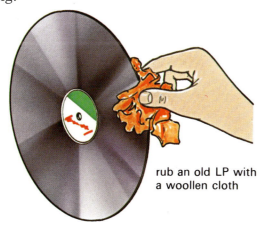

rub an old LP with a woollen cloth

glass acts as insulator

MAGIC BOATS

You will need: balsa wood • nail • paper • straw • plastic tray • magnet • cardboard • soap

These boats all work extremely well. You can make a sailing boat that can sail when there is no wind; a launch driven by soap and a jet-propelled speedboat.

Make a small sailing boat by carefully sawing a thin piece of wood into a suitable shape. Ask an adult to help if you are unsteady with a saw. Smooth the edges with sandpaper. Hammer a flat-headed nail (such as a plasterboard nail) through the wood, as shown. Stick a triangular piece of paper onto a straw, and slip the straw over the sharp end of the nail. Your boat is now ready for launching.

Fill a plastic tray with water. You can control your boat by moving a strong magnet underneath the tray. The magnet will attract the nail head under the water and drag the boat along.

Your launch can be made from thick cardboard or plastic foam packing. Wood is too heavy. Cut a notch in the stern (rear) of the launch, and wedge into it a small piece of soap. Place your launch in the water, and it will speed away.

The boat is not really propelled by the soap. The forces that exist on the surface of the water, known as surface tension, do the work. They act, or pull, around anything floating on water. The soap's job is to reduce the surface tension at the rear of the boat, which stops the surface forces pulling there. Those forces working at the front win, dragging the boat along.

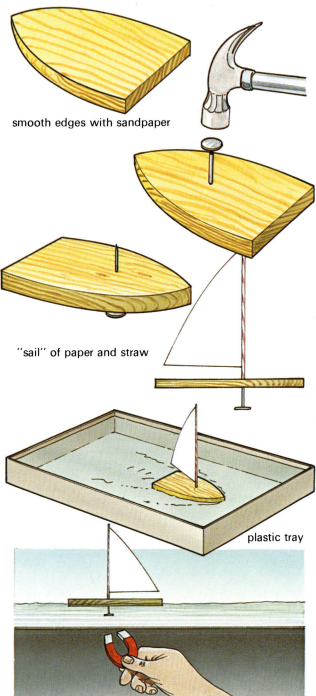

smooth edges with sandpaper

"sail" of paper and straw

plastic tray

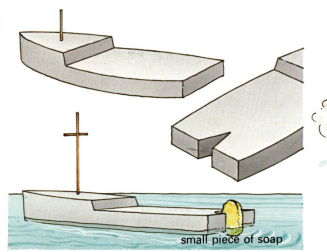

small piece of soap

STEAM POWER (X)

You will need: old cigar tube • balsa wood • nail • stiff wire • candle

Your jet-propelled speedboat will be driven by a jet of steam which you will be able to make in a boiler. For this you can use a metal tube (such as a cigar tube) or a small tin with a tight-fitting lid. Use a nail to pierce a small hole in one end of the tube (or tin). Saw a piece of wood into the shape of a boat hull and make a hole near each corner.

Make a four-legged cradle for the tube out of stiff wire. Wind the wire around both ends of the tube, and push the feet into the holes in the wood. Half fill the tube with water and fit the lid on tightly. Place a candle underneath the tube, and light it. Now launch the boat on the water, taking care not to touch the tube, which will be getting hot.

The water in the tube will soon start to boil, and a jet of steam will spurt out of the hole. As the steam escapes backwards, your speedboat will shoot forwards. It will carry on travelling until it runs out of steam.

make a cradle from stiff wire

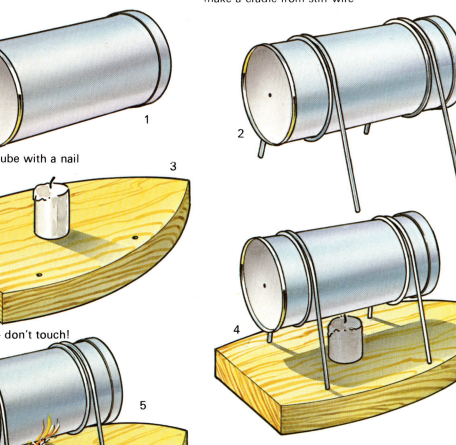

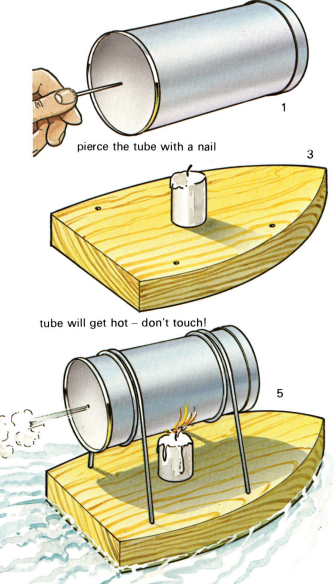

pierce the tube with a nail

1

2

3

tube will get hot – don't touch!

4

5

ACTION-REACTION

The jet-propelled speedboat works according to the law of reaction. The force (action) of the steam going backwards, sets up an equal force (reaction) going forwards, and it is this force that propels the boat. Jet planes and space rockets work on exactly the same principle.

DEEP BREATHS

You will need: 5 litre (1 gallon) plastic sweet jar ● bowl ● plastic tubing ● a friend

More than 1,000 times an hour you do something that keeps you alive. You breathe. When you breathe in, you take air into your lungs. Inside the lungs the oxygen in the air passes into the bloodstream. At the same time carbon dioxide from the bloodstream passes into the air that you breathe out. This breathing process is called respiration.

An adult's lungs can hold more than 5 litres (1 gallon) of air. Find out how much air your lungs can hold.

Fill the jar to the brim with water, and put your hand over the top. Turn the jar upside-down and stand it in a large bowl of water, so that the neck is under the surface. You may need some help – this is quite tricky to do. Take your hand away, and the water will stay in the jar. (Can you think why? Think about air pressure.) Now, tilt the jar and push the end of a piece of rubber or plastic tubing inside. Ask someone to hold the jar so that it doesn't fall over.

Take a deep breath and blow through the tube until your lungs are empty. The air from your lungs goes into the jar, forcing the water out. The amount of air in the jar after you have finished gives you a rough idea of your lung capacity – how much air your lungs can hold.

You can easily measure how much air there is in the bottle. Take out the tube and put your hand over the neck, and remove the bottle from the bowl. Turn it the right way up. Using a measuring jug, find out how much more water is needed to refill the jar. This will be your lung capacity. You should be able to increase your lung capacity by regular exercising and deep breathing.

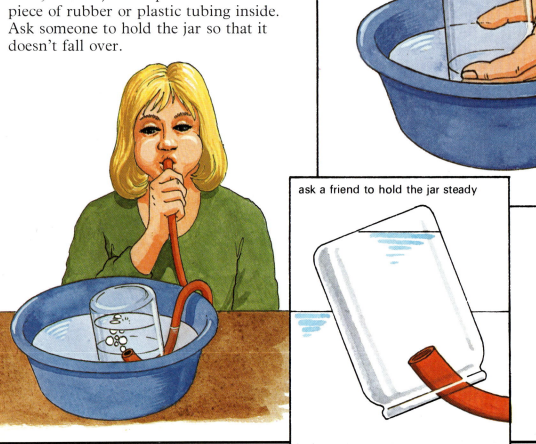

you may need help turning the jar upside down

ask a friend to hold the jar steady

HEAR YOUR HEART

You will need: 3 lengths plastic tubing • 3 funnels • y-shaped joint • a friend

When you take any exercise, you breathe faster and your heart beats faster. This gives your body the extra oxygen it needs to make energy. Find out how much faster your heart beats after exercise. You can do this by taking your pulse, but this is sometimes difficult to find. It is more fun to listen to your heartbeat with a home-made stethoscope. This works and looks much like the instrument doctors use to listen to your heart.

Make your stethoscope using three lengths of rubber or plastic tubing and three small funnels. Metal funnels are best, but plastic ones will do. Join the tubes together with a Y-shaped joint, which you can get from most hardware stores. Fit the funnels into the ends of the tubes, making sure they fit tightly.

Your stethoscope is now ready. Ask a friend to hold two of the funnels to your ears, and place the third against your chest. You'll be able to hear your heart thumping – the funnels help to magnify the sound. Count the number of times your heart beats in a minute. It can vary from 60–80 when you are not moving. How much faster does your heart beat after you have been running? And how long does it take to return to normal?

ON THE BEAT

The heart has nothing to do with love or any emotions as some people like to think! The heart is just a pump, and its job is to pump blood around the body. We feel this pumping action as the heartbeat.

Actually the heart is two pumps in one. The right side of the heart takes blood that has been around the body and pumps it into the lungs. The left side takes blood from the lungs and pumps it back around the body.

The heart is a tremendously powerful pump moving over 7,000 litres (1,500 gallons) of blood around the body every day as it beats 100,000 times.

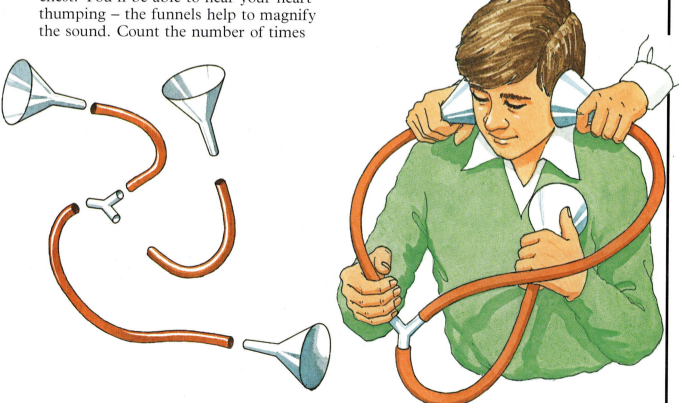

AIR PRESSURE TRICKS

THE HUNGRY BOTTLE (X)
You will need: shelled egg • clean milk bottle • newspaper • lighted taper

What do bottles like to eat? Boiled eggs! Just try this experiment.

Clean out and dry a milk bottle, which has a neck slightly smaller than an egg. Drop some pieces of crumpled-up newspaper into the bottle and set them alight with a taper. You might want an adult to help you do this. Stand the bottle upright and push the egg lightly into the neck.

The bottle needs no further bidding and greedily starts to swallow the egg whole! After a while you will notice that the burning paper goes out. And soon the egg stops moving. Perhaps the bottle has had enough.

The trick works because of air pressure. Before the paper in the bottle starts to burn, the pressure of the air trapped inside by the egg is the same as the air pressure outside. But when the paper starts burning, it begins to use up the oxygen in the air inside the bottle. So the pressure in the bottle starts to fall. The air outside is now at a higher pressure, and starts to push the egg into the bottle to make the pressures equal. This continues until the paper stops burning, showing that all the oxygen in the air inside the bottle has been used up. The egg will then stop moving because the pressure inside won't fall any lower.

YOU WON'T SPILL A DROP
You will need: glass of water • card

Turning a glass of water upside down without spilling the water is easier than you may think. Place a piece of card over the glass and holding the card in place, turn the glass upside down. Take your hand away. The card *should* keep the water in place. . . .

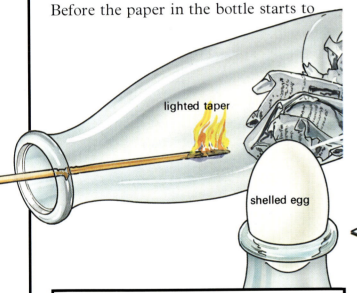

lighted taper

shelled egg

THE OCEAN OF AIR

The Earth is surrounded by a layer of air, called the atmosphere. We live at the bottom of this layer, and the air above presses down on us with a force of 1 kg on every sq cm (14.7 lb on every sq in). This is called the atmospheric pressure. If you hold out your hand, there is a force of nearly 10 kg (22 lb) pressing down on it. You can't feel it, because an equal force is pressing up on the other side of your hand, and the two balance out.

IT'S EASY TO SEE. . .

UP PERISCOPE!

You will need: 2 cardboard boxes ● 2 mirrors ● sticky tape

Submarine commanders use periscopes to look above the surface of the sea while they are still submerged. The idea behind a periscope is that a mirror high up reflects light down to another mirror at eye level, which in turn reflects the light into your eyes. For this to work the mirrors must be angled exactly at 45 degrees, or half a right-angle.

You can use two small boxes to hold the mirrors, and then tape them together to make the periscope. Make a hole for viewing in one side of each box and then tape a mirror opposite the hole at an angle of 45 degrees. Fit the boxes together so that the holes point in opposite directions. Tape cardboard lids on the top and bottom of your periscope to stop stray light from entering.

MAKE A TELESCOPE

You will need: 2 convex lens ● 2 cardboard tubes

It is quite easy to make a simple refracting telescope which will help you to look at the Moon in detail. At an optician's ask for two ordinary convex lens. One should be 5 cm (2 in) in diameter and of 92 cm (36 in) focal length. The smaller lens should have a focal length of 2.5 cm (1 in).

All you need now is a cardboard tube about 92 cm (36 in) long and about 5 cm (2 in) in diameter and a shorter tube about 15 cm (6 in) long, which will slide into the larger one. Fix the large lens at one end of the long tube, and fix the other lens, the eyepiece, in the short tube. The short tube can then be adjusted by sliding it in and out of the larger tube.

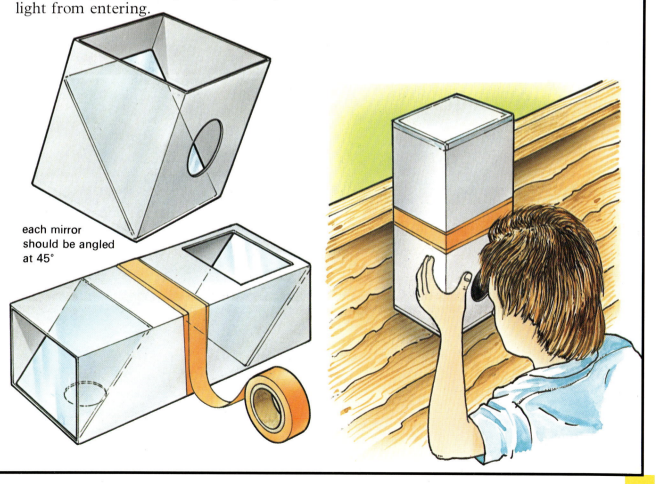

each mirror should be angled at 45°

RING TIN-TIN

You will need: 2 tin cans • twine • hammer • nail • a friend

When you speak to a friend, a pattern of sound waves leaves your mouth. These waves are vibrations, or movements back and forth, of the air. When they reach your friend's ears, they make his or her eardrums vibrate. And your friend hears what you said. If you speak quietly, your voice won't carry very far. So you'll need a phone.

Here is one you can make from a pair of tin cans and some thick twine. Use tins that had a lid, and that were not opened with a tin opener, otherwise they will have jagged edges. Using a hammer and nail, make a hole in the bottom of each tin. Thread the twine through the holes and tie a knot each end to prevent the twine pulling out.

Your phone is now ready. Give one tin to a friend and walk away from each other until the twine is stretched tight. Motion your friend to speak quietly into his tin, while you put yours to your ear. You should be able to hear what he is saying quite clearly. The stretched twine carries the vibrations of your friend's voice from his tin to yours. Remember that solid things conduct, or pass on, sound waves better than the air does and the twine is acting as a conductor.

don't use tins with jagged edges

thick twine

WATER SPINNER

You will need: cork • knitting needle • 6 pen
nibs • wire coathanger • plastic bottle • nail •
water

Some of the most powerful machines in
the world are driven by running water.
They are water turbines, the modern
versions of the water wheels our ancestors
used to produce power for grinding grain.
Today water turbines are used mainly in
hydroelectric power stations to drive the
generators which produce electricity.

You can make a small water turbine
yourself using a cork and some thick pen
nibs. First, push a knitting needle
lengthways through the middle of the
cork. Do this carefully – knitting needles
are sharp. Now stick 5 or 6 nibs into the
cork evenly spaced, so that they stick out
at right-angles. Your turbine rotor is now
complete.

Make a stand for the rotor using wire
from an old wire coathanger. Bend the
wire to form a cradle for the needle, using
a pair of pliers if necessary. (Watch your
fingers again!) Place the rotor in the
cradle, and your turbine is ready for
action.

You can make the turbine spin just by
placing it under the tap. But it can be
done more effectively using a water jet
from a can or bottle (a large plastic soft

drinks bottle is ideal). Pierce a hole near
the bottom of the bottle with a nail. When
you fill the bottle, the water spurts out of
the hole in a jet. Arrange your turbine so
that the jet strikes the rotor blades at
right-angles. Many hydroelectric power
stations have this kind of arrangement.

space nibs evenly

knitting
needle

cradle made
from wire
coathanger

A HYGROMETER

You will need: wooden stand • cotton reel • straw • human hair • drawing pin • sticky tape • card

It often rains when the air is humid, or contains lots of moisture. You measure humidity with a hygrometer.

fix cotton reel to stand

run hair round cotton reel

pin straw under cotton reel

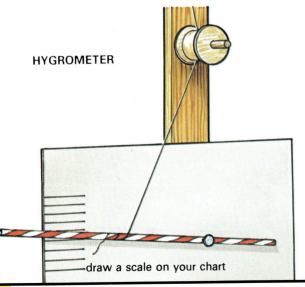

HYGROMETER

draw a scale on your chart

Ask an adult to make a wooden stand like the one shown. Find a long, blond human hair (blond hair is particularly stretchy) and fasten the hair with sticky tape to the top of the stand. Run the hair over the cotton reel.

Stick the card to the stand. Pin the straw under the cotton reel, making sure it moves freely. Pin the straw nearer one end than the other and suspend the heavy end by tying the hair round it.

You can roughly calibrate, or put a scale on, your hygrometer by noting the readings when it is near a radiator (dry, low humidity), or when it is draped with a hot wet towel (wet, high humidity).

RAIN GAUGE

HOW WATERY IS SNOW?

You will need: jam jar • snow

When there's been a heavy snowfall, it's hard to imagine what'll happen to all that water. But there is less water in a mound of snow than you might think.

Next time it snows, collect some in a glass jar. Fill it up, but don't pack it tightly. When the snow melts you'll see that you haven't got a lot of water. The snow was really ice crystals with air between them.

A BAROMETER

You will need: jam jar • balloon • elastic band • straw • glue

One of the main instruments you need is a barometer, to measure the air pressure. Stretch a piece of rubber from a balloon over the neck of a jam jar and keep it tightly in place with an elastic band. Glue the end of a straw to the middle of the piece of the rubber. This becomes your pointer.

When the pressure of the atmosphere goes down, the pressure of the air trapped inside the jar becomes higher, and pushes up the rubber. The tip of the pointer dips

BAROMETER

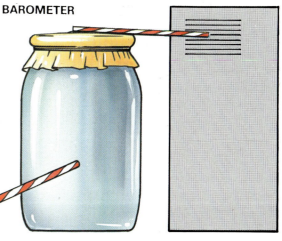

down. When the outside air pressure goes up, it presses down the rubber, and the tip of the pointer rises. When the air pressure rises, it usually means that better weather is on the way. When the air pressure falls, rain can usually be expected.

A RAIN GAUGE

You will need: large can • jam jar • rain

When rain does come, measure the amount of rainfall with a rain gauge. All you really need is a large can – a 5 l (8 pt) plastic emulsion paint can, washed out, is ideal. You could measure the rainfall directly with a rule marked in centimetres or inches. But it is better if you use a separate jar which you calibrate first.

Pour water into your rain gauge can to a depth of, say, 5 cm (2 in). Then pour the water from the can into the measuring jar – a narrow straight-sided jar is best. Divide the depth of water into equal parts, and make this your scale. When it next rains, pour the water from the can into the jar, and read the amount of rainfall from the scale.

Meteorologists can gain a lot of information about future weather from the wind. From the wind direction they can tell what kind of weather is on the way. From the wind speed, they can tell how quickly that weather is going to reach us.

A WIND VANE

You will need: cardboard • nail • glue • broom handle • drill • compass

You can make a wind vane quite simply. Cut out a large arrow from a piece of stiff cardboard, making sure it has a large tail. Carefully push a long nail smeared with glue through the middle of the arrow, as shown. Make sure it is evenly balanced.

Put the nail in a hole drilled in the top of a post (or broom handle) so that it can turn freely. Stick the post in the ground in an open space. Use a compass to find out in what direction it is pointing. Remember that a north wind blows *from* the North.

AN ANEMOMETER

You will need: 2 rubber balls • 2 pieces of wood • nails • drill • hammer • 2 washers • glue

An anemometer has a spinner, or rotor, that turns round when the wind blows. The faster it turns, the higher is the wind speed. The rotor carries a number of cups to catch the wind. For your anemometer, make the rotor cups from the halves of

two hollow rubber balls. Nail the halves to the four ends of two pieces of wood, about 40 cm (16 in) long by about 2 cm (1 in) square. Drill holes through the centre of each piece, large enough to take a long nail. Join the pieces together in the middle in a cross shape and glue them together with strong wood glue.

When the glue has set, hammer the nail through the rotor into the top of a post. But first place two large washers underneath the rotor so it can spin more freely. Stick the post in the ground in an open space. To estimate the wind speed, count the number of times the rotor spins in half a minute. If you divide this number by 3, this gives you roughly the wind speed in kph. (To get the speed in mph, divide by 5.)

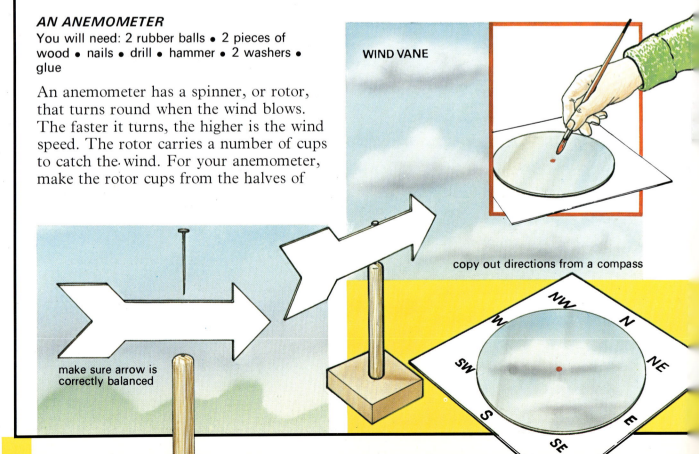

WIND VANE

copy out directions from a compass

make sure arrow is correctly balanced

NW N NE W E SW S SE

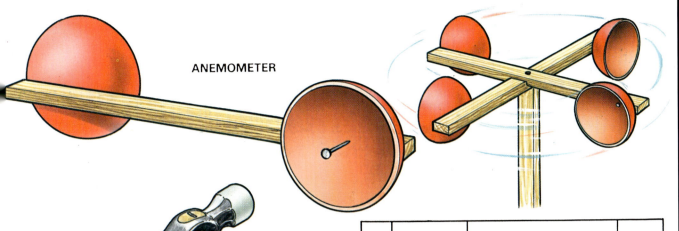
ANEMOMETER

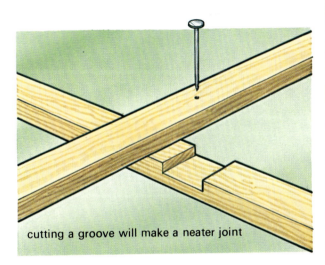
cutting a groove will make a neater joint

washers help rotor to spin freely

No	description	effect of wind	kph
0	calm	smoke rises vertically	less than 1
1	light air	smoke drifts, vane doesn't move	1–5
2	light breeze	leaves rustle, vane moves	6–11
3	gentle breeze	light flag extends	12–19
4	moderate breeze	dust and loose paper raised	20–29
5	fresh breeze	small trees sway	30–39
6	strong breeze	large branches in motion	40–50
7	moderate gale	whole trees in motion	51–61
8	fresh gale	twigs broken off trees	62–74
9	strong gale	chimney pots and slates removed	75–87
10	whole gale	trees uprooted	88–101
11	storm	widespread damage	102–120
12	hurricane	devastation	above 121

DOING IT BY NUMBERS

You can get a rough idea of the speed of the wind by observing how it affects trees and the smoke from chimneys. In 1805, an English admiral, Sir Francis Beaufort, devised a scale for wind speeds based upon similar observations.

PLOP AND GLOW (X)

You will need: 9-volt battery • 2 carbon rods • 2 test tubes • bowl of water • lighted taper

Chemists use a kind of shorthand method to describe the chemical substances they use. For instance, they refer to water as H_2O, its chemical formula. It shows that water is made up of the chemical elements hydrogen (H) and oxygen (O), and that there are twice as many hydrogen atoms in water as oxygen atoms.

You can show this to be true in a very interesting experiment, the electrolysis of water. Electrolysis is a way of splitting up substances into their chemical elements by means of electricity. In the experiment use a 9-volt battery or similar to supply the electricity. DON'T TRY TO USE THE MAINS ELECTRICITY – IT IS VERY DANGEROUS.

Wires connect the two terminals of the battery to the two electrodes, which carry the electric current into and out of the water in the bowl. For electrodes, use carbon rods taken from old torch batteries. Over the electrodes place two test-tubes full of water.

When the battery is connected, you will notice bubbles of gas rising from the electrodes. The gas collects in the top of the tubes. After a while, you will notice that twice as much gas collects in one tube as in the other. When you have collected quite a lot of gas, test it to find what it is, using a lighted taper. You may need to ask an adult to do this.

Take the first tube out of the water and immediately plunge a lighted taper inside it. There will be quite a loud "plop" as the gas inside burns up. This shows that the gas was hydrogen. Take the second tube out of the water and plunge into it a glowing, but not burning, taper. The taper will immediately burst into flames, showing that the gas was oxygen.

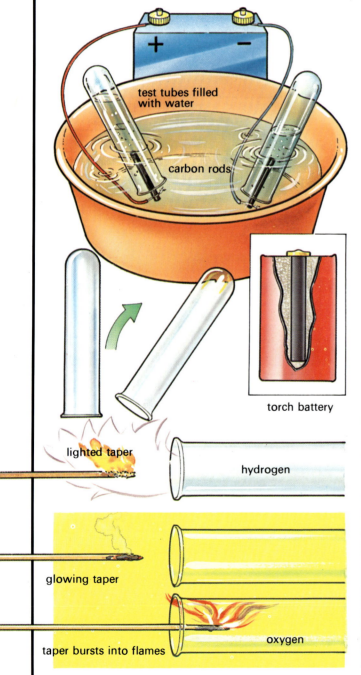

test tubes filled with water

carbon rods

torch battery

lighted taper

hydrogen

glowing taper

taper bursts into flames

oxygen

ANODES AND CATHODES

Don't forget to note which electrode gave which gas in the experiment above. The hydrogen is given off from the cathode, the electrode connected to the negative (−) terminal of the battery. The oxygen is given off from the anode, the electrode connected to the positive (+) terminal.

COMPASS NEEDLES

You will need: card • magnet • tape • needle • cork • glass of water • detergent

You can easily make a simple compass yourself, using a sewing needle as a compass needle. But first you must magnetize it. Only then will it point North – and South of course. Stick the needle on a piece of card with tape to hold it down. Then with one end of a magnet, stroke the needle from the middle towards one end about 50 times. After each stroke, raise the magnet clear of the end of the needle and come back down to the middle in a circular motion. Always stroke the needle in the same direction and with the same end of the magnet.

After 50 or so strokes, the needle will be well magnetized. Now you have to support it so that it can turn whichever way it wants, just like the needle of a proper compass. Stick the needle on or through a thin slice of cork, and then float the cork on a glass of water (with a little detergent added to the water to help it float freely.)

When you have made your cork or jar compass, you will notice that the needle always comes to rest pointing in the same direction. One end will point North, the other South. But which is which? You could check with a proper compass, but that would be cheating! Find out which end points North in the same way as your far-off ancestors did, by looking at the skies. The Sun lies in the South at midday (if you live in the northern hemisphere). So shadows point North at that time. At night you can find North by looking for the Pole Star, which lies over the North Pole.

You can fix other directions with your compass by drawing a compass card, which shows all the compass points. Slip this card under your compass.

stroke the needle with the magnet

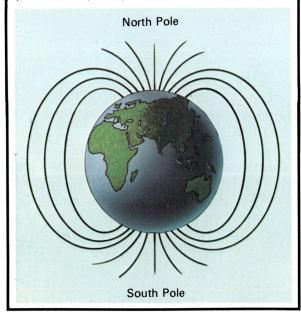

THE EARTH MAGNET

A compass works because the Earth behaves like a gigantic magnet. One end of this Earth magnet lies near the Earth's North Pole, the other lies near the South Pole. The ends of the Earth magnet attract the ends of the compass needle, so that the needle points North–South.

The ends of the Earth magnet are not exactly at the North and South Poles. Compasses point to magnetic North, more than 1,600 km (1,000 miles) away form the North Pole.

North Pole

South Pole

MAGNET MAGIC

You will need: 2 bar magnets ● cardboard box ●
lolly sticks ● iron filings ● compass

Playing with magnets can be lots of fun,
and you can learn about the laws of magnetism at the same time. You can buy
small bar (straight) magnets or horseshoe
magnets, but bar magnets are best for
these activities. You will need two.

Hang up each magnet in turn from a
piece of thread. Let them come to rest.
You will find that both magnets end up
pointing in the same direction. If you
check with a compass, you will find they
point North–South. (Why? *See page 27.*)
Mark N or S on the ends of each magnet
according to which way they point.

Place one of the magnets on top of a
cardboard box. Draw around it with a
pencil and stick ice lolly sticks along the
line. Place the magnets in the middle so
that the two N ends and the two S ends
of the magnets are together. Watch how
the top magnet floats in the air!

This shows you that two N ends and
two S ends of magnets repel, or push
against each other. If you place the top
magnet the other way round, the two
magnets will stick together. The N and S
ends of two magnets attract each other.

You can find out something else about
magnets using iron filings. These are tiny
specks of iron, which you should be able
to buy from a hardware store or hobby
shop. Sprinkle a few filings onto your
magnet. You will find that they stick only
to the ends, not to the middle. This shows
that the magnetism is concentrated near
the ends, at the "poles" of the magnet.

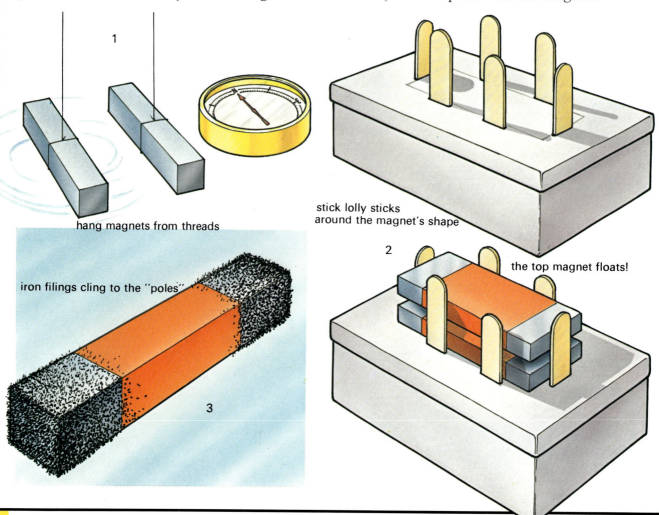

1

hang magnets from threads

stick lolly sticks
around the magnet's shape

iron filings cling to the "poles"

3

2

the top magnet floats!

MAKING FACES

You will need: card ● copper wire ● tape ● iron filings ● battery

On a piece of card, draw the outline of a face, and then follow the line with a length of copper wire. Tape it in position. Cover the wire with a piece of thin card, and sprinkle some iron filings on top. Connect the ends of the wire to a battery (NOT THE MAINS) and tap the card lightly. The face will suddenly appear.

This happens because when electric current flows in a wire, it creates magnetism. It sets up a magnetic field. The face appears because the iron filings are attracted to the magnetic field around the wire.

This connection between electric current and magnetism is very important. As a result we can make electric motors and electromagnets.

SWITCH-ON POWER

You will need: copper wire ● bolt ● battery ● switch ● paper clips

You can make an electric-current magnet using a length of copper wire and a large nail (or bolt). Wind the wire around the nail many times and tape it in place. Join the ends of the wire to the terminals of a battery through a simple switch (*see page 30*). Switch on. Bring the nail head near some paper clips and drawing pins, and watch them jump to it. Switch off the current, and the pins and clips will fall away.

By winding the wire in a coil around the nail, you have made it into a magnet when the current is flowing. But the magnetism goes when the current is switched off. We call such a magnet an electromagnet.

lay copper wire over your drawing

cover with thin card

iron filings

connect wires to a battery

copper wire

switch

battery

switched on

switched off

clips and pins jump to nail

clips and pins fall away

DI, DI, DIT, DAH, DAH, DAH, DI, DI, DIT

You will need: wood ● drawing pins ● copper wire ● tin can ● 9-volt lantern battery

Today we live in an age of instant communications. You can talk on the phone to friends in distant places. You can hear on the radio and see on the TV things happening on the other side of the world.

Until about 150 years ago there were no means of instant communications. The quickest way to send a message was by horse rider. Then, in the 1830s, Samuel Morse in the United States invented an electric telegraph. He sent messages along wires using electricity.

You can make an electric telegraph yourself with simple apparatus – pieces of wood, a few drawing pins, a long length of copper wire, two strips from a tin can and a battery. Try to use bell wire – you should be able to buy it at a hardware store or electrical shop. For the battery, use a 9-volt lantern battery or something similar.

You need to make two kinds of devices – a sender, or key, to transmit messages; and a receiver, or sounder, to receive them. Make the sender using a strip cut from a tin can. Cut it out carefully with tin snips, or ask an adult to do it for you. Pin the strip in position, as shown in the picture, but don't push the drawing pins fully in yet.

To make the receiver, nail two pieces of wood together into an L-shape, as shown. Hammer a nail into the base and wind round it about 40 turns of wire. Tape it in position. Fix another tin strip on the upright piece of wood so that one end is a few millimetres above the head of the nail.

THE MORSE CODE

A	· —	B	— · · ·
C	— · — ·	D	— · ·
E	·	F	· · — ·
G	— — ·	H	· · · ·
I	· ·	J	· — — —
K	— · —	L	· — · ·
M	— —	N	— ·
O	— — —	P	· — — ·
Q	— — · —	R	· — ·
S	· · ·	T	—
U	· · —	V	· · · —
W	· — —	X	— · · —
Y	— · — —	Z	— — · ·
1	· — — — —	2	· · — — —
3	· · · — —	4	· · · · —
5	· · · · ·	6	— · · · ·
7	— — · · ·	8	— — — · ·
9	— — — — ·	0	— — — — —

This is the code Samuel Morse worked out to send messages along his telegraph. Radio operators still sometimes use this code today. In an emergency, they send the message which is the title of this section: . . .

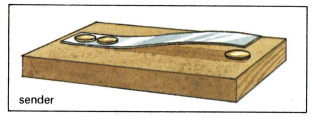

sender

receiver

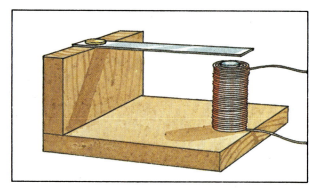

Join one end of the wire from the coil to the fixed end of the sender, and the other to one terminal of the battery. Join the other battery terminal to the drawing pin beneath the free end of the sender strip, as in the picture.

Now you can send your message by tapping the sender. When you press down, the strip makes contact with the drawing pin underneath, and this completes the electrical circuit between the battery and the coil in the receiver. Current flows through the coil and turns the nail into an electromagnet (*see page 29.*) The nail then attracts the strip above it, making a "click". When the sender is released, current stops flowing, and the nail stops being magnetic. The strip in the receiver springs away. You use these clicks to send messages in the Morse code, clicking quickly for dots, and slowly for dashes.

(see page 29.)

THE MODERN TELEGRAPH

The modern version of Morse's electric telegraph is the telex, now widely used in businesses throughout the world.

Messages are sent from one subscriber to another by code (but not Morse code), using machines called teleprinters. A person sending a message types it on a typewriter-like keyboard. The teleprinter changes the message into coded electric signals and transmits them to the receiving teleprinter. This changes the coded signals back into words, and types them out to give a printed message.

Pictures, too, can be transmitted along communications lines, using fax, or facsimile machines. The fax transmitter changes a picture into coded electric signals, and the receiver changes them back into a picture again.

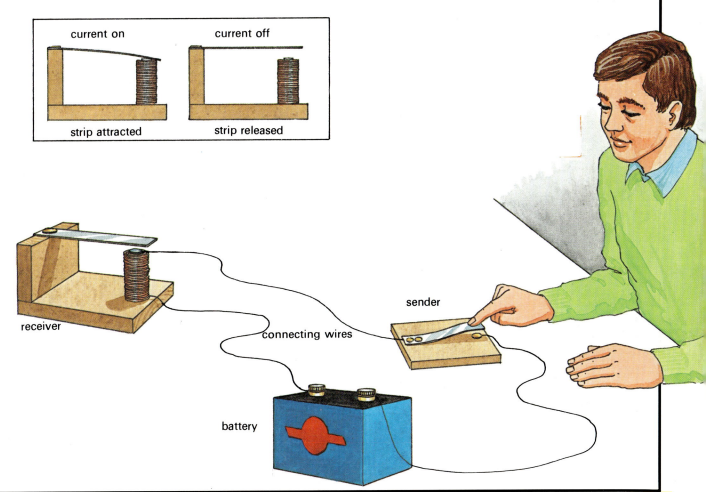

current on   current off

strip attracted   strip released

receiver

connecting wires

sender

battery

Index

Air pressure, 16, 18
  to measure, 23
Anemometer, to make, 24
Astronomy, 10
Atmosphere, 18

Barometer, to make, 23
Beaufort scale, 25
Blood circulation, 17
Boats, to make, 14–15
Breathing, 16

Carbon dioxide, 7, 16
Chemical formula, 26
Chromatography, 4
Clouds, 13
Colour, 3–5
Compass, to make, 27

Earth, 10, 27
Electric telegraph, to make, 30–1
Electricity, 12–13, 21, 26, 29–30
  hydro, 21
  static, 12–13
Electrolysis, 26
Electromagnet, 29, 31

"Fax", 31
Fingerprints, to take, 8
Fire, to put out, 7

Guitar, to make, 11

Hearing, 11
Heart, 17
Humidity, to measure, 22
Hydroelectric power, 21
Hygrometer, to make, 22

Kaleidoscope, to make, 3

Lightning, 13

Magnetism, 14, 27–9
Meteorology, 22–5
Moon, 10
Morse code, 30–1

Optical illusion, 9
Oxygen, 7, 16–17, 26

Periscope, to make, 19
Power
  steam, 15
  water, 21
Prism, 4

"Proxima centauri", 10
Pulley system, 6

Rainbow, 4–5
Rain gauge, to make, 23

Senses, 8–9, 11
Sight, 9
Snow, 23
Sound waves, 11, 20
Spectrum, 4
Stars, 10
Stethoscope, to make 17
Sun, 10

Taste, 8
Telegraph, to make, 30–1
Telephone, to make, 20
Telescope, to make, 19
"Telex", 31
Thunder, 13
Touch, 9

Water turbine, to make, 21
Weather, 13, 22–5
Wind, 24–5
  direction, 24
  speed, 24–5
  vane, to make, 24

Published in 1988 by
The Hamlyn Publishing Group Limited
a division of Paul Hamlyn Publishing
Michelin House, 81 Fulham Road, London SW3 6RB

Copyright © The Hamlyn Publishing Group Limited 1988

ISBN 0 600 55740 5

Printed and bound in Italy
Front jacket illustration: Camilla Jessel, Anwar Islam, Linden Artists
Illustrations: Linden Artists (Brian Watson, Clive Spong)
Photographic acknowledgments: Science Photo Library, Zefa
Design: Tony Truscott
General editors: Gillian Denton, Lynne Williams